Joseph Wright

PUBLISHED BY: Joseph Wright
Copyright © 2016 All rights reserved.

Table of Contents

Introduction

Congratulations on buying, "Retirement Planning: Plan your 30 year retirement in 30 minutes". This book will show you the essential factors you need to consider in order to plan the retirement of which you have always dreamed.

Many of us spend a lot of time thinking about the paradise of retirement – a time free of the demands of work, the obligations of being somewhere at a particular time and the demands of an unappreciative and unreasonable boss. We sacrifice our time and commitment today in order that we may have a prosperous and lengthy retirement when we can finally do exactly what we want, whenever we want.

Unfortunately, far fewer of us dedicate any time at all to plan how we are actually going to reach this wonderful state of existence. We know the desired destination – we just don't know how we are going to get there. We're not even sure where to begin or even where to start to look to find out. Many of us are either too busy with the pressures of everyday life to begin to concern ourselves with how our life is really going to look when we actually retire. It is as if we have embarked on an important journey with no map, no guide and no provisions – just a blind hope that somehow, in the fullness of time, we will safely find our destination.

This book will both answer your questions and also show you some of the aspects of your current life you should be examining in order to ensure your life in retirement is as comfortable and prosperous as possible. It aims to show that this should not be a frightening process but one that should excite you and give you assurance that even very small steps taken today will have great benefits later on.

It is not a book that is jam-packed with technical jargon and page after page of technical statistics which make this vitally important process entirely inaccessible to most of us. I hope this book gives you a solid understanding of the main questions you should be asking yourself and the different aspects of retirement to consider in a format that is easily understood. I am sure that when you have finished you will feel more comfortable about your own retirement plan and ready to take those few steps that will place you on the right path to ensuring a solid, financial future for decades to come.

This book is not going to cover every single aspect of retirement planning in minute detail – indeed, no such book could even be written, such is the size of the topic. What it will do however is give you the motivation to start saving today for your retirement, the confidence to believe that you can do it and the understanding of how important today's actions are for your future.

In summary, I hope this book becomes that map and guide on the road to the happy and wealthy retirement that you deserve. Read on to plan your 30 year retirement now.

Chapter 1 – Understanding your position

When to start retirement planning

The rather frightening answer to this question is "the day you started work" or possibly even earlier however the vast majority of us do not start thinking about retiring and providing for ourselves as we get older until that day looms large on the horizon. Before then, we may prioritise other obligations such as housing or providing for a growing children,, seeing the world or buying a car. We may have viewed retirement as something for other people to worry about, a chore for the generation up to be getting on with, a job that we probably should be thinking about but there was always something else, just a little more interesting to do at precisely the right time. Therefore, the realistic answer for when you should start must be – "today".

Survey after survey reveals that the vast majority of people have insufficient plans in place to provide them with the lifestyle they hope to have on retirement. It also shows that people vastly underestimate exactly how much money they might need to leave the life they want and that over a third of people have given no time to plan a rewarding retirement whatsoever.

Around 30% of US households have less than $10,000 in liquid assets, that is, money they could use to invest to provide an income. A further 24% have between $10,000 and $99,000. That's over half of Americans who do not currently have enough money to produce an income to retire on. The projected poverty figures make bleak reading with over a quarter of Americans facing life in retirement in near-poverty. Those who fail to make any kind of retirement planning or provision were found to have the greatest likelihood of living in extreme poverty once they have left work. The message is very clear – recognise that retirement is inevitable and start to put some plans in place right now that will cover the vast percentage of your working income once you have retired.

The good news however, is that it is not too late to start and that the plans you put into place today are going to pay off handsomely over the coming years. Even if you have already retired, there are still many steps you can take in order to squeeze every last amount of potential from your savings and even to increase them.

What kind of life do you want to have in retirement?

Many people look forward to retiring their entire life. They go to work to a job they dislike, dreaming of the day when they can stop and put their feet up. Unfortunately, many people do little more than that and have no real idea of the kind of life they would like to lead. They have no idea of the goals they might have or the places they might want to go or the things they might want to do. For many, retirement can come as a huge shock and present difficulties of its own. What do you do all day? If you are in a relationship, can it adjust to the two of you being around each other all the time? What is it like not to have a pre-defined purpose or some kind of structure to your day?

Take a moment now to think about what you want to achieve. Think about the goals you might set and how you hope to live your life in accordance with the values you hold dear. Do you envisage a big change to your life? Will you live in the same home for example? If you want to travel, how often do you see that happening? Will life in retirement be more or less the same without the necessity of going to work or do you see yourself with a part-time job or volunteering for example?

Perhaps you have talents or interests that due to the pressures of work you were unable to fulfil during your career. Did you long to be an artist or an author or a sports coach or do charity work but never found the opportunity? Are you a musician who would love nothing more than the chance to practise throughout retirement and play in a group or put on a concert?

If you are in a relationship, then this is something that you should discuss together. Many relationships suffer a shock later on when two people have a vastly different idea of how they will spend retirement. Have a conversation between you so you can identify common goals and aspirations and also areas of possible conflict later on. It is far easier to commit to financial planning when both parties are working for a common cause. Financial arguments are a common cause of discord between couples and it's best to find out what each of you would like before embarking much further on this journey.

What do you need in retirement?

It is also crucial that we think about what we are going to need to survive on a day to day basis. What are the absolute essentials to a safe and healthy retirement today? How much are they going to cost?

Many of the actual figures will vary from household to household of course, however let's consider some of the common factors that will affect us all. You should make a rough estimate for now of how much you think it will cost you. The factors below are those considered the most important by the Health and Retirement Study. This is a project which surveys Americans every two years on their retirement spending.

Housing

A general housing bill will probably be your largest expense in retirement. You should factor in any mortgage interest or charges you think you might still incur, property maintenance and insurance and the various utilities. You will still be liable for all of these as you were in your working life. The percentage of your income spent on housing will decrease as you get older and the mortgage is fully paid off, however the maintenance and utilities costs will continue to increase. It is most likely this will be your greatest expense in retirement.

Food

You will have a rough idea of how much you spend on food at the moment (we will talk about budgets later) which may depend on whether you are feeding any dependents as well. Eliminate the cost of eating out for the time being and focus only on how much it would cost to feed yourself on a monthly basis. Bear in mind also that as you are retired you will have more time to cook for yourself without buying more expensive pre-prepared meals so you may find this expense cheaper.

Transportation

The good news here is that you will no longer be paying to get to work so you can expect your transport costs to drop considerably. Chances are however you will still have an automobile so will need to factor in gasoline, insurance, maintenance and repairs. Even if you favour public transport that will still have an annual cost attached ($500).

Health care

The cost of health care can go up of course in retirement, more so if you were forced to retire on health grounds. When you account for insurance, drugs and medical services in general it might be around $5000 a year.

Clothing

This should be another area where savings can be made in comparison to those you incurred while working. You will no longer have to buy expensive suits to look the part in the office or at meetings however your clothes will of course wear out over time. Clothing will probably make up the smallest percentage of your expenses at around 3%.

Durables

This category would include replacing a car or refrigerator, washer, dryer, dishwasher, television and other such items. While not absolutely essential to surviving, life would be far more uncomfortable without any of these devices and at some point they will need replacing. You can expect to spend around 6% of your income on these durable items.

What would you like in retirement?

Thinking back to your list of targets above should prompt you now to think about those things you would like to have or activities you would like to do in your retirement. If you would like to be more musical for example you will need the instruments and some lessons. If you would like to develop your artistic side, you will need the relevant equipment. If you want to take lots of trips there will be significant expenses here. I have included two further categories here under this section because although you do not critically need them to survive it is quite likely you will spend money on them and you should factor them into your planning now.

Entertainment

This would cover going out to eat, tickets to particular events or the cinema, any hobbies you might have, cable TV or Netflix or similar services, internet subscription charges, cell phone charges and anything else you think you might use for your own entertainment.

Gifts

Gifts are an obvious, but often overlooked category, when it comes to planning. Include here any gifts you think you might give to family or friends and also any charitable donations.

Make an accurate list

Make a list of all of the above expenses and put down the associated cost you estimate you will have to pay. Factor in that you will not have dependents and that certain costs, as mentioned above, will be far less in retirement than in working life. For reference, you will find that housing and food will probably be your two greatest costs making up over a third of your total costs on an annual basis.

Think again about what kind of life you would like to lead in retirement – does it involve travel? Expensive hobbies? What kind of talents and interest would you like to develop? How much of an effect on your finances might they have? Of course, you may not know the figures exactly but for the time being have a rough estimate of the type of numbers that will be involved.

By looking at these figures closely we can begin to understand exactly how much money we are going to need, firstly just to survive in relative comfort and secondly in order to live the life we want to lead when we retire. These, along with your life expectancy which we will look at later, are the key factors in determining how large your total pot of money needs to be before you can retire comfortably. Once we know that figure, we can look at ways of reaching that figure faster and perhaps increasing the comfort levels of retirement still more.

Summary

- It is never too early or too late to start making plans for your retirement. Start today. Start now.
- Plan for those things in life you are going to need.
- Have an idea of how much money you will need monthly, both for things you need and the type of life you would like to lead in your retirement.

Chapter 2 – Close the Gap

Unless you have already been diligent in saving and put into place a solid retirement plan it is likely that your projected expenses of retirement are not yet going to be adequately covered by your retirement funds. If they are, then congratulations and well done! Nonetheless, it is worth reading ahead still as additional funds earned now will have hugely beneficial effects in lowering your potential retirement age. Every dollar you earn today will earn you that amount several times over in the years to come. If you want to have enough for the luxuries in life on retirement or if you would like to retire earlier than your peers, you need to action right now.

There are two ways that we can try and achieve our aims– we can either get more money somehow or we can spend less and therefore save more money from our existing income. In an ideal world, we can do both and see the gap close even faster than we might have thought possible.

Earning more

Let's look at the idea of earning more first of all. There are many ways of gaining a side-income which can provide a big bonus upon our usual earnings. We will still have to pay tax on this income however even an extra few dollars can make a big difference once it starts to compound over a long time. Here are a few avenues you could think about exploring in order to get that extra money coming in. Think about what your current skill set is and how you could use that outside the work place to forge an extra income. If you have an interest or skill in something you might be surprised how easy it is to use that and how much people are willing to pay you to solve a problem for them

Build a website

If you are involved in technology or the Internet at all you might be adept at building a website. Use that to create a site that refers your visitors to buy particular products. If you don't feel your web-building skills are up to scratch just yet, then use a pre-defined template such as WordPress and create a blog. Choose a topic that is of genuine interest to you and to which you will be able to add valuable content – give your viewers a reason to keep coming back and listening to what you are saying.

For example, if you are interested in running you could talk about your preparation for running races in terms of practice runs or diets or equipment. You could make a post every week and put up your times and practice sessions. You could then advertise particular pieces of equipment or foods or any other resource that would be of value to runners. You may not make millions but you could certainly make extra cash on the side just writing about a topic you are already knowledgeable about and enjoy.

If you are really interested in a particular area that is quite narrow, a niche topic for example, you will find some like-minded people who are eager to hear what you say as there may not be much existing information already. For instance, you could talk about running for men over 50 or running for people with little time or any other narrow topic about which you feel you could offer value.

Food

A broader area, but if you are a great baker or cook in general perhaps you could leverage this skill and provide catering for friends or family or local businesses. This is a huge area where people are happy to pay for someone else to do the work and a very decent side income can be gained here with a little application.

Coaching

Look at your areas of expertise and consider how they could benefit other people who need the knowledge you have. You can offer this in the local community or you could expand still further and offer skype calls over the Internet for example for an hourly fee. There are also sites that will handle all the infrastructure for you in terms of the call and financial backend such as clarity.fm where you are able to offer expert one-on-one advice for a fee.

Buying and selling

Take a look around you and note those things you no longer use or have simply lying in a drawer gathering dust. Get them out and put them on craigslist or eBay for a profit. This has the added advantage of being paid to declutter your own house. Once you've done that you could continue to check Craigslist and pick up the bargains to resell later for a further profit.

Dog walking

If you have some spare time you can take pets out for exercise and get fit at the same time. There are plenty of people who are willing to pay for their dog to get some exercise as they are too busy to get to do it themselves.

Driving / taxi work

This could be an activity at night or the weekend. There are plenty of services where you can sign up and drive your own car (Uber is perhaps the most well-known) and earn yourself a wage driving people around. The infrastructure is handled by the companies who will take a cut of the earnings themselves.

Freelancing

This is something you can offer people, again over the Internet, which could well be in your current line of work. If you are a graphic designer or a writer or a programmer for example you could offer exactly the same service but on a freelance basis.

Here are a few more jobs that you could do to earn extra money:

- Decorating
- Cleaning service
- Modeling
- Mystery Shopper
- Online surveys
- Personal trainer
- Pet groomer

- Pet sitter
- Photography
- Proof-reader
- Rent out a room
- Music teacher
- Translator
- Gardener

This is not an exhaustive list – there are many, many others. It's not the purpose of this book to go through every single opportunity however the point is there are hundreds of possible ways to earn more money doing things you are already doing for fun anyway. The money you are earning is going to go a long way to providing you with a lot of extra money in your retirement.

Saving money

Another extremely easy way to generate more savings cash is to cut down on your spending. Just as a business is continually looking for ways to be leaner and more cost-effective to enhance its profits, you should look at ways to do the same. In order to do this, I would very strongly encourage you, starting today, to make a budget of your expenses.

In a spreadsheet write down everything you spend. If you have a partner record what you are both spending. Account down right to the last penny where your money is going. Every cup of coffee or meal out or little present should be noted down. Once you have a month's worth of data or even a couple of weeks you can begin to see where your funds are disappearing. It is critical that you keep this budget to be at least aware of where your money is going. It may be you want to buy five lunches a week out but you must at least be aware of how much it is costing you both today and in the future.

When you have an accurate record of the money being spend, sit down and see where the saving can be made. What kind of savings can you make? Do you need cable TV? Netflix? Help around the house? Expensive meals out? What can you do yourself today that is going to help your future self out?

Have the right mind-set

It is important to have the right mind-set when dealing with saving. Far too many of us view saving with horror, as if it is some kind of depravation that is going to prevent us living life to the full or enjoying ourselves at all. In reality, the opposite is true. For example, if you are determined to save money by cooking yourself rather than eating out all the time or buying pre-prepared meals you are gaining not losing. You are gaining a life-long skill in cooking or baking your own food that is going to save literally tens, if not hundreds of thousands of dollars, over your lifetime. You are gaining an insight into how food is prepared and an appreciation of where food comes from and its real value. You are probably going to be eating much more healthily which in turn is going to have a huge effect upon the quality of life now and in your later years. You may well cook with your partner or family or friends giving you a further opportunity for family time or socialising which you could not get otherwise. You may well in turn pass on these cooking skills to your own family who will also gain further benefits for themselves.

We could look at another example of saving money through travel. Using the car less will have huge financial benefits and if we make more of an effort to walk the health benefits here will be very significant. If we don't want to walk we could get a bike. This again is highly beneficial both financially and health-wise and might allow us to get to parts of our local town or city that we might never have seen otherwise. We may even be able to combine some of these money-saving activities with money-earning side jobs essentially allowing us to make money even while we are saving it.

We all know about avoiding the small expenses in life and how quickly these things add up. The coffee from the café around the corner is of course the most famous example. A coffee every working day might save you $5 a day or $25 a week or well over a $1000 a year. If you take that over 10 years and then factor in the interest you have earned on the money you are now not spending, you are well into a five figure saving over the course of your working life. Over a period of 10 years for example you will save over $16,000. That's $16,000 closer to your target meaning you can either retire earlier or have a more comfortable retirement when you do retire.

Think big and think small

Having said that, cutting a coffee a day is not going to be the be all and end all of your financial planning and saving. Consider every aspect of your saving – both big and small. Naturally, all of these little savings add up to very substantial savings over time, but don't just look at minor issues in day to day life. Consider the much broader aspects too. As we have already seen, housing is going to be the single most expensive outgoing cost you have in retirement. Consider trying to reduce the cost of housing now.

If you are renting, perhaps you could share with a roommate or continue to do so a little longer than you thought you might have to. If you are thinking of buying a house, consider the size of your prospective home. How big an area will you genuinely need to be comfortable? The size of the house doesn't just affect the initial cost of course, but all of the subsequent utility costs and maintenance which will be more expensive the bigger the house is. Consider the area – is there somewhere cheaper you might be able to relocate to? Somewhere with public transport links perhaps or within cycling distance of work?

Borrowing money

One additional way you can save a huge amount of money in the long run is to defer your need or expected pleasure from buying something slightly in order to eliminate the need to borrow money. Borrowing money comes at a cost, often a very expensive one, and although there are times which it is unavoidable or perhaps even absolutely necessary, such as a mortgage for a house, for the vast majority of purchases you should strive your utmost to avoid it.

Let's take one example – the seemingly constant need that advertising pushes upon us to change our car, to get the latest model, to get rid of a vehicle that is working perfectly well to replace it with the newest, flashiest version. Even if we put aside the fact that buying a new car is a huge expense and one which starts to depreciate immediately, at least if you can buy it from money that you have saved you are not incurring the additional expense of paying more for the privilege.

When you take out a loan to buy a car you are being hit with huge additional interest charges which you are going to have to pay for several years to come. Indeed, many people never rid themselves of this debt at all and once they have owned their new car for three years will rush to upgrade it, taking on even greater debt in the process. In doing so they are depriving their future selves of income, of spending power, of money that could have been set aside to bring retirement closer and plug that gap we discovered earlier in the book.

Maybe you borrow the money from a credit card or a personal loan or some kind of hire/purchase agreement from the car dealer. By buying that expensive, fully-loaded car when you are younger you are punishing yourself in the future. You are not borrowing from anyone else but yourself – you are the one who will be paying the price. This goes for any item you choose – your younger self may gain some temporary pleasure from this latest purchase but it is your future self who will pay the price for having to work many years more. Remember also that all of that interest you are paying is money that also could have been invested to make even more money and bring that retirement age even closer.

Compounding Interest

We have already mentioned that the earlier you start planning for retirement the better. This is because in your younger years, time is on your side. If the stock market takes a dip for a couple of years or longer, you are in a position to wait it out. You can afford to invest and forget, confident in the long term prospects of your investments. Even if in a downturn, you are still able to save money which can be compounded, potentially over decades to ensure an excellent return.

Let's look at this wonder of compounding interest more closely. As you may know, compound interest simply means that you are earning interest on the interest that you have already earned. This means if you start saving at 20 for example you will earn interest for far longer and in turn therefore earn interest on the interest that you have already gained.

Here is a graph which shows annual contributions of $5000 to a savings account for a period of 35 years. The blue line shows the total value of the account. The orange line shows you the total value of the contributions over this time.

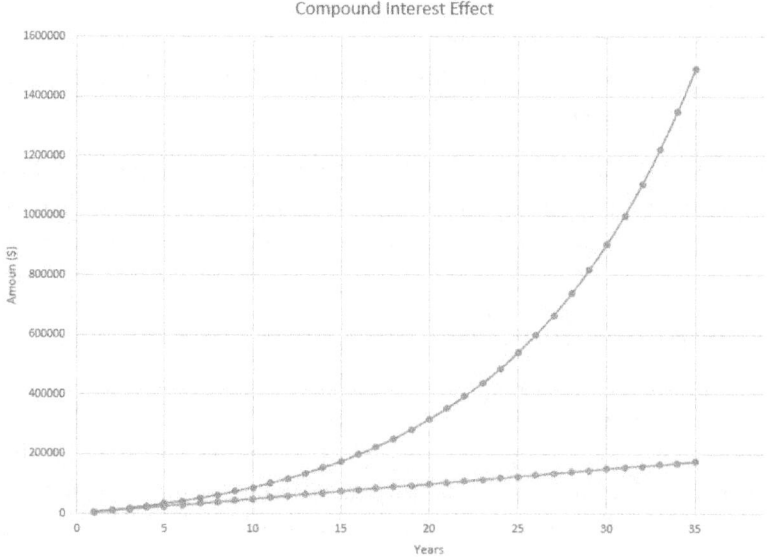

We can see that in 35 years, with a 10% savings rate, the total account is worth over $1,500,000 however the total contributions have been only $175,000. The compound interest effect here has been enormous as year after year you continue to earn interest on interest.

The same effect can be seen from a graph of two people who start saving the same amount, but at a different age. One person, Bill, starts saving at the age of 25. He contributes $250 per month over a 35-year career. His savings earn an average of 6%. Another person, James, contributes exactly the same amount, $250 per month, and also earns 6% on average, however starts 10 years later. Look at the graph below to see how these 10 years have made a difference. Bill is the blue line and James is the orange line.

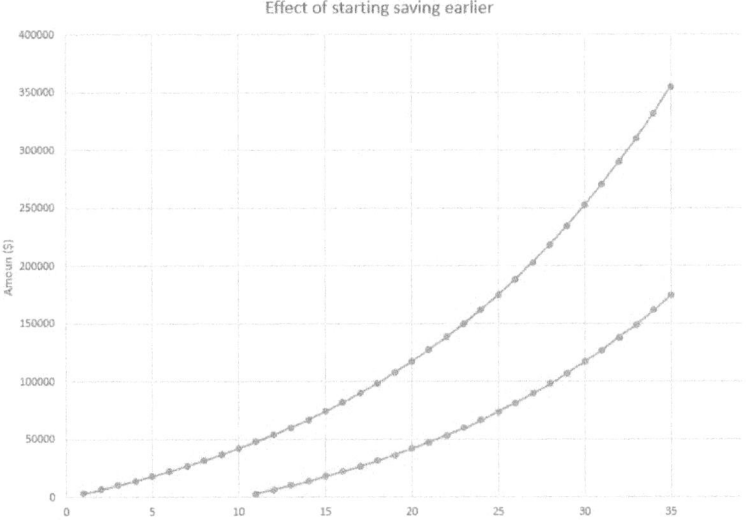

Although this doesn't seem a huge difference at first glance, by the end, Bill will finish with over $350,000 while James will end on $175,000. Despite contributing only $30,000 more than James, Bill has finished with double James' final amount with an extra $175,000. Those extra ten years have had a hugely beneficial compounding effect.

Summary

- In order to be better off we need either to earn more money or save more money (or both).
- The right mind-set is critical for saving money – little things make a big difference.

- When you borrow money you are depriving the future you of spending power.
- Start saving early and use the power of compound interest for your own benefit.

Chapter 3 - Saving Vehicles

401 (k)

This is one savings vehicle which you should be thinking hard about investing into. If you are not aware of the basics of the 401 (k) this is an employer-sponsored, defined-contribution plan. This means that many employers will match your own contributions at least in part. It also has significant other advantages with tax breaks because your own contributions are made before your taxes are deducted. This in turn will lower your taxable income and therefore the amount of tax you have to pay. Furthermore, you don't pay any taxes each year on any capital gains you may have or share dividends or any other money that you gain through your 401 (k). You should check with your employer about the participation rules. You may be delayed from contributing straightaway or the employer might delay making their own contributions until you have worked there a certain amount of time. You can always verify this with the employer. The contribution rate from the employer can vary from 25% up to 100% up to a certain amount of your pay. A common program might 100% of the first 6%. For example, if you earned $40,000 and contributed $2400 your employer would add that same amount. If you contributed only $1200, then the employer would do the same. In this case you by failing to add in the remaining $1200 on your side you are essentially losing a free $1200 from your employer. In 2016 the maximum contribution you can make is $18,000

Bear in mind that although you are allowed to withdraw money from your account the cost for doing so is an expensive one. If you are aged less than 59 ½ years, you will pay a penalty and you should try your best to avoid doing so. You will have to take the money at 70 ½ unless you are continuing to work full time.

If you leave your current employment, you can put the money into your new employer's plan or place all the funds into an Individual Retirement Account (IRA) as detailed below. Although you can withdraw the money you will then have to pay income tax on that amount as well as the early withdrawal penalty as well as losing all the benefits that your account has.

The 401(k) is an extremely valuable tool to a comfortable retirement and the first place you should look at very carefully when considering you financial planning.

IRA (Individual Retirement Account)

IRAs are retirement accounts that you can pay into that provide significant tax benefits. In a traditional IRA your contributions are tax-deductible (money deposited before tax) and any earnings you make are free from tax. When you retire and begin to withdraw from the traditional IRA this will be treated as income and taxed whatever rate applies to you. The distributions from this type of account must being at the latest by April 1 of the year after you turned 70 ½.

With a Roth IRA however the contributions you make are made from income that has already been taxed. There is no age limit applied to when you can make these contributions and the maximum allowed is $5,000. If you withdraw the money held in a Roth IRA once you are over 59 ½ and have had the money there for more than five years, there is no tax applied. There is no mandatory withdrawal with a Roth IRA.

Most people open IRAs by themselves and then invest in stocks or bonds or funds – think of it essentially as a tax-shield or wrapper upon your investments.

Social Security

Chances are you will receive some form of social security retirement benefit. What is even more likely is that it will not be enough to have the sort of retirement you would like to have. It is difficult to say exactly how much you will get as it depends primarily on how much you earned over your working life and then at what point you start collecting it. To find out how much you are going to get there are a couple of resources from the government that will help.

Have a look at www.ssa.gov/planners/benefitcalculators.htm which has a number of calculators on them to give you a rough estimate. There is even more information there for married couples and further guidance on how taking the money before retirement age will affect you.

You can also have a look at your personal statement, assuming you have set one up. Try www.ssa.gov/myaccount if you have not done so already to get one. This personal statement should give you the details on how much you will get with your current salary at different age points.

The longer you can wait to claim your Social Security the more you will be able to claim. If you can wait until you are 70 you will get 8% extra per year. On the other hand, if you need to take it earlier, before your full retirement age of 66, you will lose at least 5% a year. This is further reason to ensure you are in a good position not to need to take your Social Security payments early.

Annuities

An annuity is a type of insurance product essentially and does form part of the planning for retirement for many people. It might be worth considering if you are certain you want a steady income once you get to retirement. You make an investment now, which you hope will grow, in order that it can be paid out later in retirement. The frequency of payment might be monthly, quarterly, annually or perhaps one lump sum. How much you will get depends on how much you have invested and for how long. You can also decide if you want payments for a set time or for the rest of your life. If you take a fixed annuity you get a guaranteed, set amount. If you choose a variable annuity however the amount you get depends very much upon the performance of the annuity's investments.

Bear in mind that another factor that effects how lucrative an annuity can be is the expense associated with running these type of products. These are often high and you should make absolutely sure you know how much the financial advisor or firm is going to charge. Over time, this can have a hugely detrimental effect to your eventual pay-out.

Stocks

Stocks are simply a stake in the company that you buy. You become a small part owner in the company. If the value of the stocks goes up, you can sell them and make a profit. Until you sell your stocks, none of your profit or loss has been crystallised however. You can only actually realise your profit when you sell your stocks. You will also gain income from the dividends that the company issues, if it chooses to do so. Many people simply re-invest these dividends back into the stocks to build up their income still further.

Bonds

A bond is another form of investment which can be issued by companies or the government. You loan your own cash to whichever organisation is issuing the particular bond and in return for the risk you have taken and the time without your money you are paid interest when the bond matures.

Stock Index Funds

You can buy individual stocks however you might also consider investing in an index which will track various indexes across the world to give a balanced investment across all locations and all sectors. Some funds might get very specific by targeting small companies or large companies only or emerging companies for example. These type of funds can often have quite small investment charges which will allow you to invest more rather than spend it on financial advisors who may not gain any particular improvement anyway. By investing in low cost index funds you can increase your profit and also spread your risk over a wide variety of stocks rather than just concentrating on a handful.

Cash

People often prefer to keep at least some of their funds in cash, if not all, in the hope that the interest they earn while it is held in the bank will provide a useful return in retirement. They might feel nervous or apprehensive about investing in the stock market or other forms of investment and want to stick to the comparative safety of cash. This is certainly one option however do remember that the cost of inflation will continue to erode the value of cash. Although you are not experiencing as much volatility with your money it is possible to earn more with stock market investments. Of course, you also run a greater risk with this, so you should assess how you feel about risk before investing. It may well be a balanced approach with the bulk of your funds in cash is what allows you to sleep well at night.

Getting the mix right

As you get older of course your ability to tolerate losses diminishes because you have less time to recover if things go wrong in the stock market for example. If the value of your stocks plummets the day before you come to cash them in after decades, you may be compelled to take the loss as you have no other form of income. When you are much younger, you can be hopeful of relying on the stock value increasing in the long term. Bonds are less volatile however they will generally not offer as much of an opportunity to make long term profit as stocks. Cash remains the safest asset class to be in with the lowest volatility however it will also have the lowest return. As you get older you may need to adjust your asset allocation the closer you get to retirement.

Summary

- There are lots of different products to use to help you on the journey.
- Use the tax breaks you get from the government for extra help.
- Have a broad focus with a mix of investments.
- Think about the products that you are comfortable with even if that might mean losing some profit.

Chapter 4 – Not running out

The main concern you should think about in your retirement planning is how long you will be able to survive with the funds you have. If you are going to start cashing in your stocks for example, what would be a safe rate at which you can use your funds in order to live the life you want. If you don't intend to leave anything behind in your estate, then you want both to spend every last penny you have but also have enough in order to see you through what will hopefully be a long and happy retirement. As you don't know exactly when you are going to die, a safe spending rate can be rather difficult to predict and model. The last thing you want to happen is to get to 90 years old and then realise you have no money left. On the other hand, dying with hundreds of thousands of dollars left that you could have spent during your life doesn't seem a great option either.

Living Longer

As a race and society in general we are living much longer than we used to. Recent figures from the Society of Actuaries show that the average 65-year-old man will live for a further 21 years while a 65-year-old woman will live, on average, for another 23 years. As this is only the average figure then clearly there will be around half the people who live even longer with many making it well beyond 90 years of age. We therefore need some kind of rule to work on if we are going to strike the balance between having enough money to keep us going for possibly 30 years or more of retirement yet also being able to enjoy ourselves at the point we stop work.

The 4% rule

One of the more common pieces of retirement advice that is given today is the 4% rule. Simply put, you should spend no more than 4% of your total funds per year. If you have $600,000 across your various asset allocations you would therefore spend, at the most, $24,000. Some people are now suggesting that this 4% figure is overly optimistic and that due to diminishing stock market returns or low interest from the banks that you should be spending less than 4% each year. They point to the tech crash of 2000 and the global financial crisis of 2008 as evidence that portfolios can shrink very rapidly and have a terribly adverse effect upon retirees who do not have the luxury of taking a longer term view. Nonetheless, extensive research has found that the majority of people will actually finish with more money than they started with at the beginning of their retirement with a 4% drawdown rate.

Inflation

Another very important factor that will have a significant effect upon your savings and lifestyle will be inflation. A high rate of inflation in retirement will dramatically affect how much you are able to spend. The Federal Reserve Board has managed to limit inflation since the early 1990s back down to around 3% but you might recall the 1970s where it even managed to get into double figures. You can use inflation calculators to work out the equivalent value of money now compared to a previous date.

Bear in mind that for your investments to be successful you will need them to have returns above and beyond that of inflation. For example, if your cash is giving you a nominal 3% return you might think this is a good result however if inflation is running at 5% in real terms you have actually lost money. This is without even factoring in the potential effect of taxes! This is another reason to consider a mixed allocation of asset classes. Inflation is very hard to beat especially as there is nothing you can do to control it. It is very important however that you are aware of it and factor in the inflation rate to your calculations and financial planning. Don't ignore it and think about continuing to invest or stay invested during your retirement to combat the adverse effects inflation will have on your savings

Backcasting

The best strategy to use with your drawdown rate is to start conservatively and to be in a position to adjust it each year. You could start with just a 3% rate if you are really concerned about running out of cash and perhaps delay that trip or live a little more conservatively than you first thought you might. If you are some way off retirement at the moment this might give you cause for thought to perhaps work an extra year or two than you first thought so you have that extra buffer of money when you retire.

If we take an example with some numbers, we can "backcast" and work our exactly how much we think we will need to survive. Let's imagine that we say we will need $40,000 a year, in addition to what we will get from Social Security in order to have the retirement we want. We will therefore need a total portfolio of $800,000 in order to facilitate that retirement lifestyle. You can work out the figures yourself here and the total amount will depend on how much you think you are going to need and at what rate you end up drawing down on your portfolio.

Unfortunately, we are talking about the future so although we can look back at all the years for which we have historic data and draw our own conclusions we cannot be absolutely sure about how much we will need and for how long. However, somewhere around the 4% mark is a good place to base your initial projections and figures upon for your own retirement.

Sequence of returns

One factor that is often ignored by retirees is the sequence of your returns. It is not simply the average return from your investments that is going to have a significant impact on your financial well-being – it is also the timing of when those returns arrive. It is true that two retirees with the same amount of wealth can have significantly different financial outcomes depending on the point at which they start to take their money out from the investments. The sequence of returns is irrelevant if there are no cash flows in or out of your portfolio – it makes no difference if your portfolio has returns of +20% one year and then -20% the next or the other way around, you will still finish on the same number. However, it does have a big impact once you start introducing cash flows out from your portfolio.

For example, if you are forced to take money from your investments in order to live at a time when the stock market was down in value you would need to sell more of you funds in order to get that fixed amount of money. If the stock market remains low for five years, you are going to have to continue to remove more of your investments from your pot in order to survive. If we imagine that after five years of being low, the stock market then picks up enormously and shoots up 20% a year for the next five years your gains are not going to be as significant because your overall investment has been diminished.

Let's look at an example with figures to illustrate. If you were to have an investment portfolio of $100,000 but for some reason you need to withdraw $20,000 at the end of the first year. In one scenario the stock market falls 50% in Year 1 and then goes up by 100% in Year 2. Here we would now have to take our $20,000 from the remaining $50,000 at the end of Year 1 leaving us with $30,000. In Year 2 this sees a rise of 100% so we finish with $60,000.

However, if the 100% rise occurs at the end of Year 1 we would take our $20,000 away from $200,000 now leaving $180,000. Year 2 sees the drop of $50,000 so we would now finish with $90,000 - $30,000 more than the first example with the figures the other way around.

Clearly, these are very extreme examples but it shows that if we are in a position where we are withdrawing money we cannot just rely on the average return but have to factor in the sequence of returns as well. We can do nothing to effect change on the stock market or global economic issues, but it is something to be aware of and to factor in when deciding upon your asset allocation as you get older and decide on your preferred initial rate of withdrawal. You would want to avoid, if at all possible, making major withdrawals from your portfolio for example when the stock market is in decline and try and defer that major purchase until values have risen again and the impact upon your savings of a large withdrawal is lessened.

Summary

- You could be retired a very long time – pace yourself and your withdrawals.
- Remember the destructive power of inflation on your savings and seek to stay invested.
- The sequence of returns is important for your financial position. Having a low withdrawal rate will help see you through potentially challenging situations.

Chapter 5 – In retirement

Withdrawing money too early

The decisions about when to take your money are critical for your financial planning. If you are thinking about retiring early, then you should think very carefully about taking your cash early. Your Social Security payments will be reduced if you do not wait until the full retirement age and there will be taxes to pay from your retirement account distributions as well which you should think about avoiding. Withdrawals from your IRA for example before the age of 59½ will be subject to federal and state income tax. Think about possibly working part-time or perhaps downsizing in order to bridge this temporary financial gap and eliminate the need to take your money.

Taking your money too late

It is also very important that you don't leave it too late to withdraw your money from your tax-deferred accounts like an IRA or 401(k). The government is very keen that you start spending that cash rather than leaving it as inheritance so will impose a penalty on you for not withdrawing. These are called Required Minimum Distributions (RMDs). You have to start taking money out by April 1 of the year that follows the calendar year in which you reach 70 ½ years.

Even if you don't want to take the money out it is very unwise to leave it in the accounts as you are going to have to pay a heavy price. You will face an excess-accumulation tax which is 50% of the amount that you were required to take out. For example, if you were supposed to have taken out $5000 and fail to do so you will be taxed $2500.

Remember this does not include money kept in a Roth IRA which can stay there as long as you want. You also don't have to collect from your 401(k) or a company pension if you are still working.

Money in an IRA however will have to be taken or you will face the 50% levy.

You should consult with the IRS as to the exact minimum withdrawal amount you will need to make in order to avoid this tax. They have a series of calculations which are based on age. The calculations will tell you the exact percentage amount you will have to take.

Of course, you don't have to spend the money you withdraw. You can re-invest it or place it in a bank or give it away to a charity if you like. You will pay no tax on charitable donations if it goes straight to a charity. The government is interested in finally collecting the tax on this money which you very sensibly deferred possibly decades ago. What you do with the money once this tax has been paid is entirely up to you.

Carry on saving and investing

We have already talked about the 4% rule and how much you can withdraw safely per year to give you a long and safe retirement. Try and keep up that savings habit you have established previously though and continue to invest wisely. The good financial habits that you have ingrained into you throughout your working life still make sense now. Remember, you are potentially going to be retired for a very long time, perhaps 30 to 40 years – almost as long as your working life! If you are planning on big trips to big ticket items, then plan carefully to avoid them falling close together in the same year for example. Continue to save where you can and re-invest that sensibly just as you did throughout your working life.

Stay physically active

One of the best ways to save money in retirement is to stay active and to ensure you remain physically in good shape. Fitter people have far less chronic diseases such as diabetes, heart disease which means your ongoing medical expenses should be far less. In addition to that, the activities can be very cheap to practice such as simply going for a walk or taking a bike ride.

Avoiding an overly sedentary life will lessen the chances of putting on weight as well which in turn will reduce your health costs. There is no reason to push yourself too hard, particularly when you first retire, but making every effort to stay physically fit has a large financial upside in addition to significant health benefits.

Stay mentally active

Staying physically active will also promote being mentally fit. Exercise will get your heart pumping more vigorously which in turn will carry more nutrients and oxygen to the brain. We know that physical exercise is also key in helping with depression and various other forms of emotional distress. Being mentally active will also aid with memory. Here is a short list of mental exercises you could use in retirement:

- A crossword or puzzle once a day
- Reading more – perhaps in a book club?
- Mind games such as chess or bridge
- Take up new interest or rekindle old ones e.g. gardening
- Start a new course or even go back to school for a degree
- Go out with friends to the cinema or theatre or an art gallery
- Do some charity work with involves social interaction

All of these activities will keep your brain and mental agility at its peak which again has hugely beneficial financial effects.

Be socially active

In addition, the social interaction of these activities will help in avoiding depression and other forms of mental health. It will help to avoid loneliness and has been proven to have beneficial physical effects as well. Keeping relationships going and forging new ones in your retirement with a different set of people is important, even if it is via email or chatting over the phone. You want to stay as vibrant and active as you possibly can for as long as you can to enjoy all that financial planning you have made over the years!

Summary

- Time your withdrawals from tax-protected investments carefully.
- Stay active physically and mentally.
- Keep your social connections to stay healthy and improve your financial situation.

Chapter 6 – Conclusion

Planning for retirement can seem a daunting exercise at first. Many people find the idea of it all so overwhelming that they continue to put it off and delay until before they know it their own retirement is just around the corner. At that point, they may well regret not putting into place just a few basic safeguards to ensure they will be able to have the retirement they have looked forward to for decades.

In reading the book I hope I've been able to show that it does not have to be complicated or frightening and that little steps taken early enough can have hugely beneficial financial benefits later. The earlier you start the better off you will be however it is never too late to start to plan. You can gain some huge advantages just by knowing your available options and taking advantage of the tax breaks that are offered to you by a government that is still keen to encourage people to plan for their own retirement.

There is currently much debate about the exact financial vehicles might be best for people to use in retirement. Should you invest in the stock market or should you go for an insurance product? It is justifiable to expect the stock market to provide the greatest returns in the long run however the variance and the risk is also going to be greater. As we have seen above, the sequence of returns can have a significant effect on exactly how much you have left over. Those that think investing is the best way to go also hold doubts about the strength of insurance companies or bond issuers and their financial offerings. What if you were to invest for decades only to find the company has disappeared when you go to claim?

On the other hand, you may feel that you can trust the biggest insurance companies or bond issuers have been around for decades are already proven their financial might. If they were to default on what is owed, we would be in the middle of a far greater financial disaster which would have already seen the collapse of the stock market anyway. You may feel you would much rather have a guaranteed return that you can accurately rely on each month instead of harboring an overly optimistic belief that the stock market will eventually provide a greater return. If you are happy with what you are going to get, why would you want to risk it all for money you may not even get around to spending?

This book is not designed to tell you the answer to where exactly you should invest – the answer is probably in the middle with a combination of various financial products ranging from safe investments in a bank account up to the riskier single stock investments perhaps. Where exactly you fall in this debate will very much depend on personal preference and even your own character. You must ultimately choose a path which is going to allow you to sleep comfortably at night. You should be safe in the knowledge that you have done the required research and that, with full knowledge of the facts, you have a financial plan that you are happy with.

I hope this book has shown to you, in a clear way, two man things. Firstly, why it is so important to get a solid, financial plan and stick to it. Secondly, the various financial products and services that are available to you to ensure you have a long, secure and indeed healthy retirement.

Reading a book on retirement shows you are looking to plan ahead and ensure your own retirement will be as happy and financially sound as possible. I congratulate on starting on this most important journey to financial well-being wish you a very long, prosperous, healthy and happy retirement.

www.ingramcontent.com/pod-product-compliance
Lightning Source LLC
Chambersburg PA
CBHW070423190526
45169CB00003B/1392